The Songs of Richard Rodgers

Low Voice

Edited by Richard Walters
Bryan Stanley, assistant editor

On the cover: John Marin, *Pertaining to Fifth Avenue and Forty-Second Street,* Oil on canvas,1933.
The Phillips Collection, Washington D.C.

ISBN 978-0-634-03247-9

WILLIAMSON MUSIC®
The Rodgers & Hammerstein Organization:
A Concord Music Company

EXCLUSIVELY DISTRIBUTED BY

Visit Hal Leonard Online at
www.halleonard.com

World headquarters, contact:
Hal Leonard
7777 West Bluemound Road
Milwaukee, WI 53213
Email: info@halleonard.com

In Europe, contact:
Hal Leonard Europe Limited
42 Wigmore Street
Marylebone, London, W1U 2RN
Email: info@halleonardeurope.com

In Australia, contact:
Hal Leonard Australia Pty. Ltd.
4 Lentara Court
Cheltenham, Victoria, 3192 Australia
Email: info@halleonard.com.au

Contents

Biography

Richard Rodgers' contributions to the musical theatre of his day were extraordinary, and his influence on the musical theatre of today and tomorrow is legendary. His career spanned more than six decades, and his hits ranged from the silver screens of Hollywood to the bright lights of Broadway, London and beyond. He was the recipient of countless awards, including Pulitzers, Tonys, Oscars, Grammys and Emmys. He wrote more than 900 published songs, and forty Broadway musicals.

Richard Charles Rodgers was born in New York City on June 28, 1902. His earliest professional credits, beginning in 1920, included a series of musicals for Broadway, London and Hollywood written exclusively with lyricist Lorenz Hart. In the first decade of their collaboration, Rodgers & Hart averaged two new shows every season, beginning with *Poor Little Ritz Girl*, and also including *The Garrick Gaieties* (of 1925 and 1926), *Dearest Enemy*, *Peggy-Ann*, *A Connecticut Yankee* and *Chee-Chee*. After spending the years 1931 to 1935 in Hollywood (where they wrote the scores for several feature films including *Love Me Tonight* starring Maurice Chevalier, *Hallelujah, I'm A Bum* starring Al Jolson and *The Phantom President* starring George M. Cohan), they returned to New York to compose the score for Billy Rose's circus extravaganza, *Jumbo*.

A golden period followed—golden for Rodgers & Hart, and golden for the American musical: *On Your Toes* (1936), *Babes in Arms* (1937), *I'd Rather Be Right* (1937), *I Married an Angel* (1938), *The Boys from Syracuse* (1938), *Too Many Girls* (1939), *Higher and Higher* (1940), *Pal Joey* (1940), and *By Jupiter* (1942). The Rodgers & Hart partnership came to an end with the death of Lorenz Hart in 1943, at the age of 48.

Earlier that year Rodgers had joined forces with lyricist and author Oscar Hammerstein II whose work in the field of operetta throughout the '20s and '30s had been as innovative as Rodgers' own accomplishments in the field of musical comedy. Oklahoma! (1943), the first Rodgers & Hammerstein musical, was also the first of a new genre, the musical play, representing a unique fusion of Rodgers' musical comedy and Hammerstein's operetta. A milestone in the development of the American musical, it also marked the beginning of the most successful partnership in Broadway musical history, and was followed by *Carousel* (1945), *Allegro* (1947), *South Pacific* (1949), *The King and I* (1951), *Me and Juliet* (1953), *Pipe Dream* (1955), *Flower Drum Song* (1958) and *The Sound of Music* (1959). The team wrote one movie musical, *State Fair* (1945), and one for television, *Cinderella* (1957). Collectively, the Rodgers & Hammerstein musicals earned 35 Tony Awards, 15 Academy Awards, two Pulitzer Prizes, two Grammy Awards and 2 Emmy Awards. In 1998 Rodgers & Hammerstein were cited by Time Magazine and CBS News as among the 20 most influential artists of the 20th century and in 1999 they were jointly commemorated on a U.S. postage stamp.

Despite Hammerstein's death in 1960, Rodgers continued to write for the Broadway stage. His first solo entry, No Strings in 1962, earned him two Tony Awards for music and lyrics, and was followed by *Do I Hear a Waltz?* (1965, lyrics by Stephen Sondheim), *Two By Two* (1970, lyrics by Martin Charnin), *Rex* (1976, lyrics by Sheldon Harnick) and *I Remember Mama* (1979, lyrics by Martin Charnin and Raymond Jessel).

No Strings was not the only project for which Rodgers worked solo: as composer/lyricist he wrote the score for a 1967 television adaptation of Bernard Shaw's *Androcles and the Lion* for NBC; contributed songs to a 1962 remake of *State Fair;* and to the 1965 movie version of *The Sound of Music*. He composed one ballet score *(Ghost Town,* premiered in 1939), and two television documentary scores: *Victory at Sea* in 1952 and *The Valiant Years* in 1960 (the former earning him an Emmy, a Gold Record and a commendation from the U.S. Navy.)

Richard Rodgers died at home in New York City on December 30, 1979 at the age of 77. On March 27, 1990, he was honored posthumously with Broadway's highest accolade when the 46th Street Theatre, owned and operated by the Nederlander Organization, was renamed The Richard Rodgers Theatre, home to The Richard Rodgers Gallery, a permanent exhibit in the lobby areas presented by ASCAP which honors the composer's life and works. The centennial anniversary of Rodgers' birth in 2002 was celebrated all over the world with renewed attention on the composer's vast output.

Editor's Preface

The Songs of Richard Rodgers is an earnest and serious attempt to present the work of the greatest of American theatre composers as vocal literature. When surveying art song, opera, theatre music, and all sorts of popular genres, it becomes clear that as lasting, performable vocal music, the enormous body of musical theatre literature is at the very center of our American vocal heritage.

This selection of Richard Rodgers songs was made by answering one primary question: Which songs are most vocally gratifying? Rodgers was a master of especially lyrical melody, consistently writing tunes that naturally sing. But since a book of 900 songs wouldn't be practical in the least, choices were painfully necessary. Some attention was given to the fame of individual songs in the selection process, particularly in the Rodgers & Hart output. Another important factor was the viability of the song as a solo. The varied talents of different types of singers was also considered.

This edition is designed for singers of all types. Teachers and singers coming from a traditional vocal studio perspective will be served particularly well.

Most of these songs have never before been published in transposed keys. Choosing keys is tricky business. Typically, in this genre of music, a tenor is vocally flattered in a key a step above the ideal soprano key. If a soprano is asked to sing too high in most Rodgers songs, it is difficult for her to find the optimally expressive use of the lyrics. The choice of key in the High Voice edition ultimately took the gender of singer into consideration, as well as making a judgment about which key would serve the most people.

The keys for the Low Voice edition presented different challenges. Classically defined mezzo-sopranos may sometimes be best accomodated in a relatively high key, or in some songs might prefer a more of a sultry, belting range. Indeed, a lyric mezzo-soprano ideally may want to own both the High Voice and Low Voice editions, and make a vocal choice on a song by song basis. While this Low Voice edition was not conceived with belting as its only objective, this was a factor in choosing keys. Some songs are clearly not, by nature, for belters anyway. However, for appropriate songs a typical belting range was considered.

Baritones tend to sound best in lyrical theatre music in the most medium of ranges, not going too low or too high. Basses, on the other hand, obviously like a lower range. Each song presented its own vocal world in choosing the published key. As in the High Voice, considerations were made of the gender of the implied singer, with an aim at providing vocal comfort for the most typical voices.

There are two songs in the collection that are not transposed. Billy Bigelow's expansive "Soliloquy" from *Carousel*, which is really an aria, only appears in the Low Voice edition. "My Lord and Master" from *The King and I*, so suited to a soaring soprano range in its Puccini-like climax, has not been transposed, and only appears in the High Voice edition.

This is as pure a presentation of the music as is possible, but still accomodating the purpose of a singer and accompaniment edition. We have respected the harmonizations and original Piano/Vocal editions of the songs that Rodgers himself approved, but also have adapted them. Piano/Vocal sheet music is designed as much as a piano solo, with the melody in the piano part, as for singing. For this new edition, we have instead adapted accompaniments. The book includes no outright free arranging, however.

I'll leave the interpretive suggestions to the many teachers, coaches and directors out there. I'll only remind the singer to choose the song insightfully and prepare it lovingly. Not every song flatters every voice and temperament. But in the enormous expressive range of Richard Rodgers, any singer can find more than a few songs to last a lifetime.

RW

Bewitched
PAL JOEY

Words by LORENZ HART
Music by RICHARD RODGERS

This is the original show lyric. Hart fashioned a standard lyric that appears most often in print, and can be found in other publications.

Climb Ev'ry Mountain

THE SOUND OF MUSIC

Lyrics by OSCAR HAMMERSTEIN II
Music by RICHARD RODGERS

Do I Love You Because You're Beautiful?

CINERELLA

Lyrics by OSCAR HAMMERSTEIN II
Music by RICHARD RODGERS

Edelweiss
THE SOUND OF MUSIC

Lyrics by OSCAR HAMMERSTEIN II
Music by RICHARD RODGERS

Falling in Love with Love

THE BOYS FROM SYRACUSE

Words by LORENZ HART
Music by RICHARD RODGERS

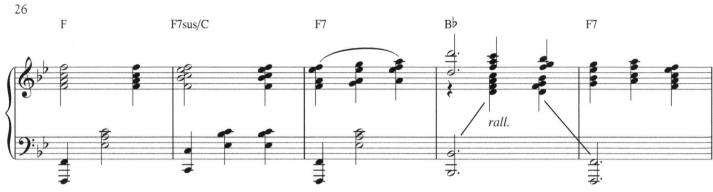

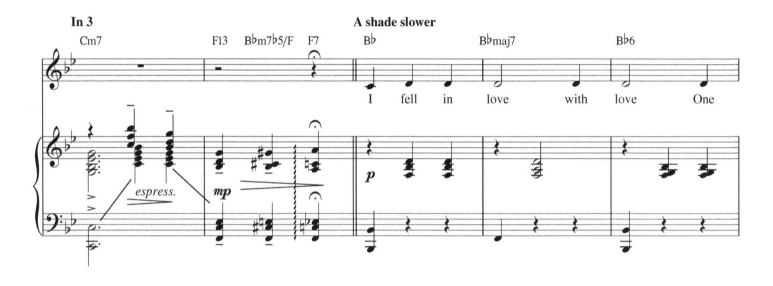

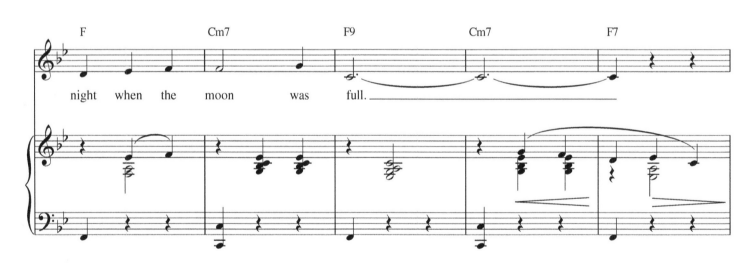

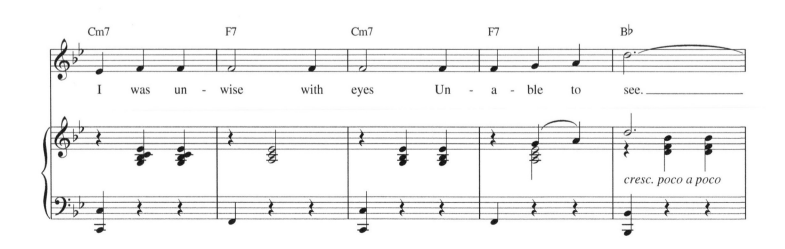

Hello, Young Lovers

THE KING AND I

Lyrics by OSCAR HAMMERSTEIN II
Music by RICHARD RODGERS

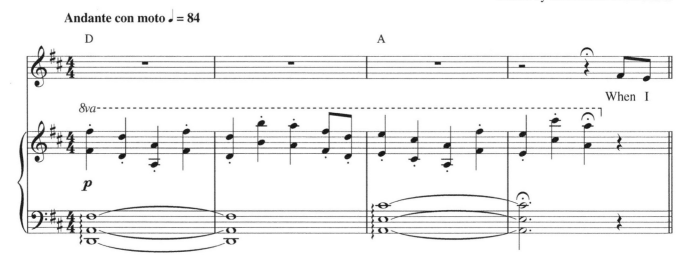

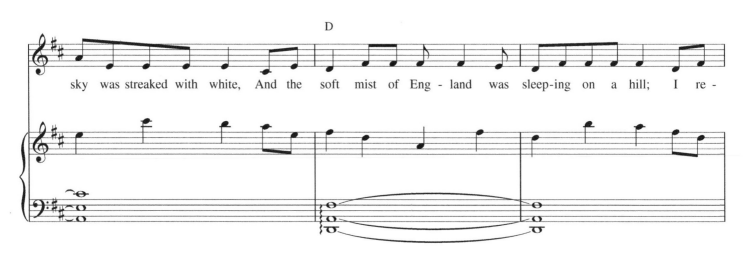

hope your trou-bles are few. All my good wish-es go with you to-night

poco rit.

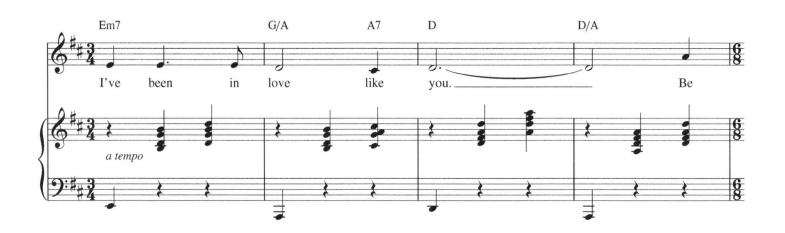

I've been in love like you. _____ Be

a tempo

brave, young lov-ers, and fol-low your star, Be brave and faith-ful and true,

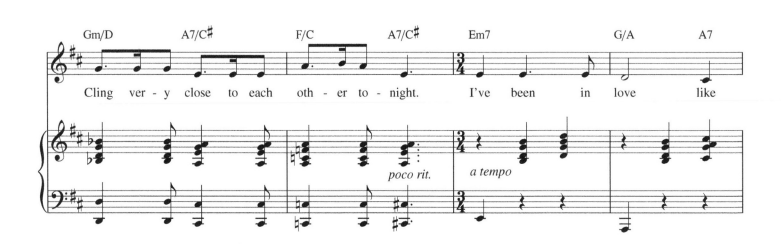

Cling ver-y close to each oth-er to-night. I've been in love like

poco rit. *a tempo*

I Wish I Were in Love Again
BABES IN ARMS

Words by LORENZ HART
Music by RICHARD RODGERS

I Could Write a Book

PAL JOEY

Words by LORENZ HART
Music by RICHARD RODGERS

I Didn't Know What Time It Was

TOO MANY GIRLS

Words by LORENZ HART
Music by RICHARD RODGERS

I Have Dreamed

THE KING AND I

Lyrics by OSCAR HAMMERSTEIN II
Music by RICHARD RODGERS

If I Loved You
CAROUSEL

Lyrics by OSCAR HAMMERSTEIN II
Music by RICHARD RODGERS

Allegretto moderato

Both Julie and Billy sing this song in the show, each with a different version of the verse.
There is a spoken line for Billy, said during the introduction: "I can just see myself."

Isn't It Romantic?

from the Paramount Picture LOVE ME TONIGHT

Words by LORENZ HART
Music by RICHARD RODGERS

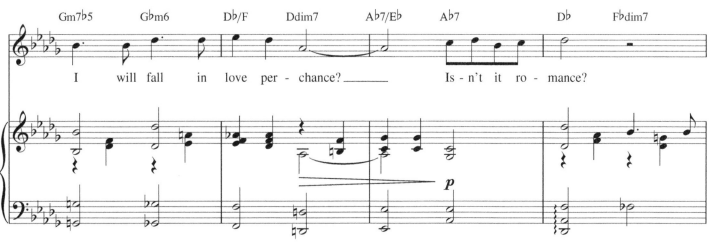

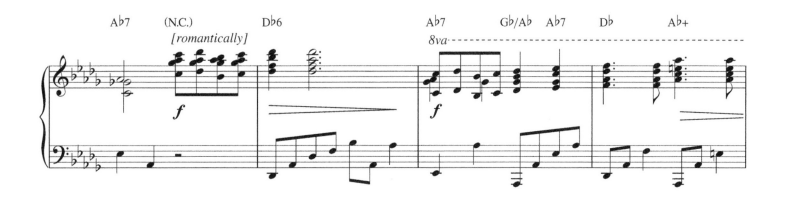

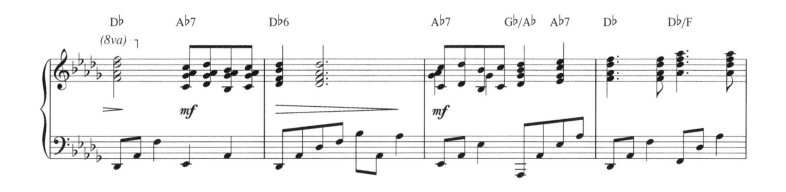

It Might as Well Be Spring

STATE FAIR

Lyrics by OSCAR HAMMERSTEIN II
Music by RICHARD RODGERS

It Never Entered My Mind

HIGHER AND HIGHER

Words by LORENZ HART
Music by RICHARD RODGERS

With tranquillity

I don't care if there's pow-der on my nose, I don't care if my

hair-do is in place. I've lost the ver-y mean-ing of re-pose, I

nev-er put a mud-pack on my face. Oh, who'd have thought that I'd

walk in a daze now, I nev-er go to shows at night, But just to mat-in-ees now.

I see the show and home I go.

poco rit.

REFRAIN
Slowly, with warm expression

Once I laughed when I heard you say - ing That I'd be play - ing

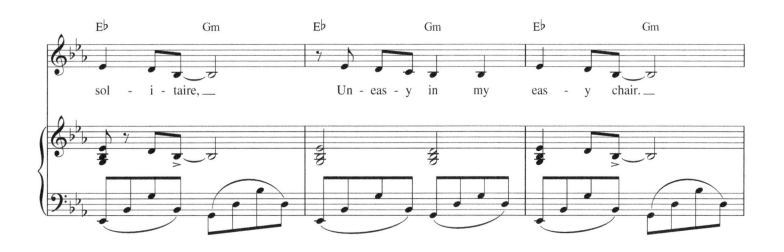

sol - i - taire, Un - eas - y in my eas - y chair.

The Lady Is a Tramp

BABES IN ARMS

Words by LORENZ HART
Music by RICHARD RODGERS

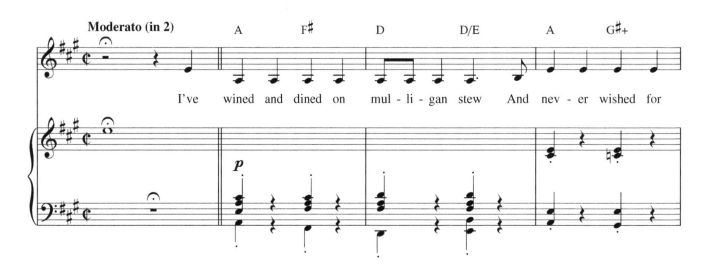

I've wined and dined on mul-li-gan stew And nev-er wished for

tur-key, As I hitched and hiked and drift-ed too From Maine to Al-bu-

quer-que.___ A-las, I missed the Beaux arts ball And what is twice as

Love, Look Away
FLOWER DRUM SONG

Lyrics by OSCAR HAMMERSTEIN II
Music by RICHARD RODGERS

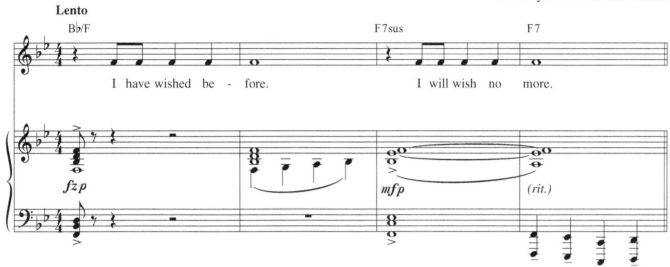

I have wished be - fore. I will wish no more.

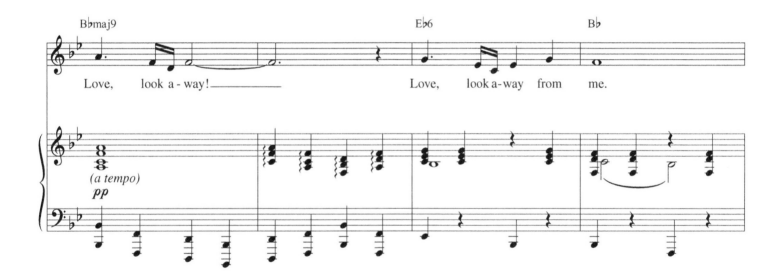

Love, look a - way! Love, look a - way from me.

Fly, when you pass my door, Fly and get lost at sea.

Manhattan
from the Broadway Musical THE GARRICK GAIETIES

Words by LORENZ HART
Music by RICHARD RODGERS

81

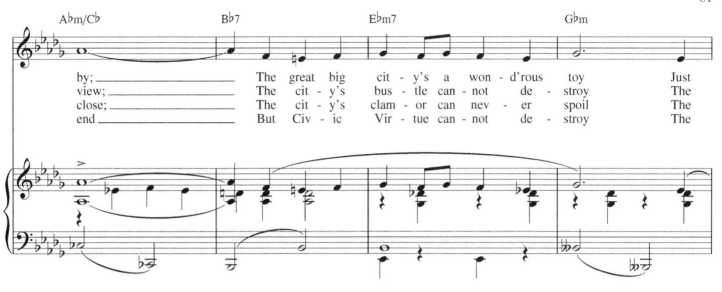

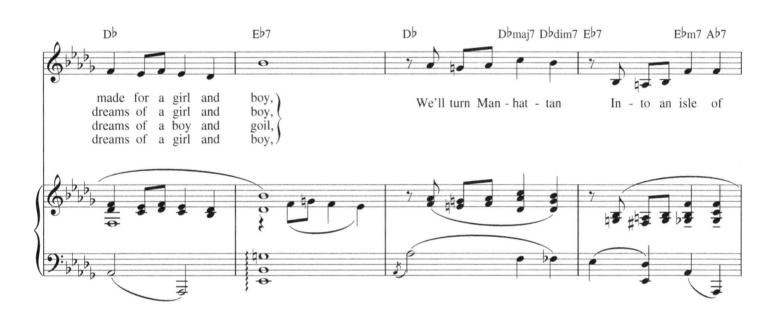

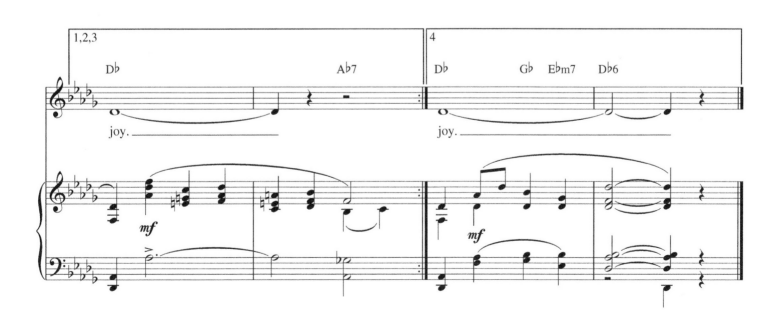

My Favorite Things

THE SOUND OF MUSIC

Lyrics by OSCAR HAMMERSTEIN II
Music by RICHARD RODGERS

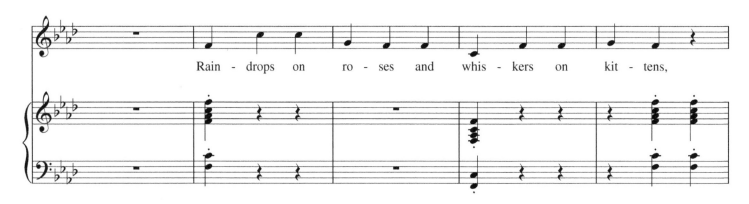

Rain - drops on ro - ses and whis - kers on kit - tens,

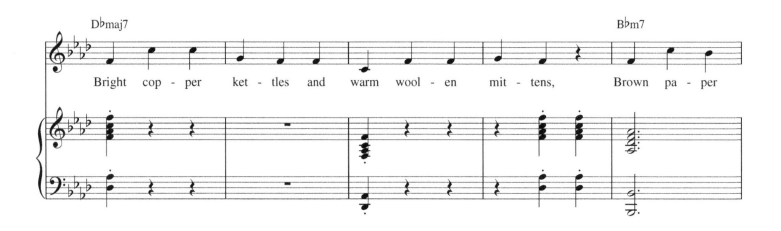

Bright cop - per ket - tles and warm wool - en mit - tens, Brown pa - per

D♭maj7   B♭m7

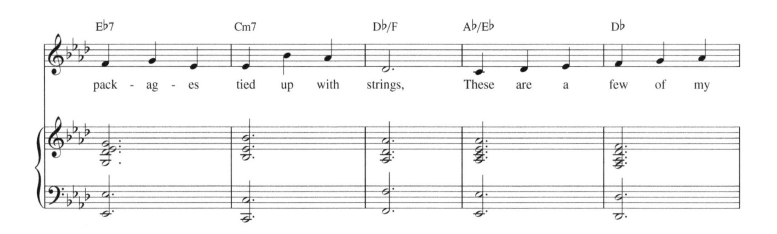

pack - ag - es tied up with strings, These are a few of my

E♭7   Cm7   D♭/F   A♭/E♭   D♭

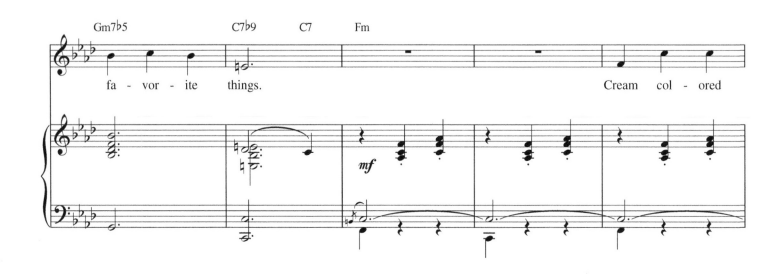

fa - vor - ite things.   Cream col - ored

Gm7♭5   C7♭9   C7   Fm

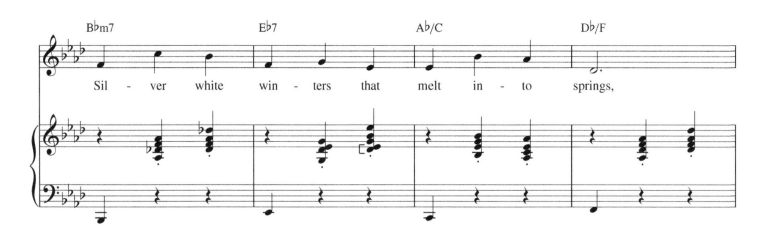

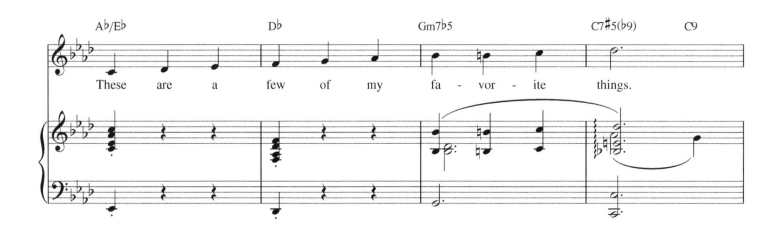

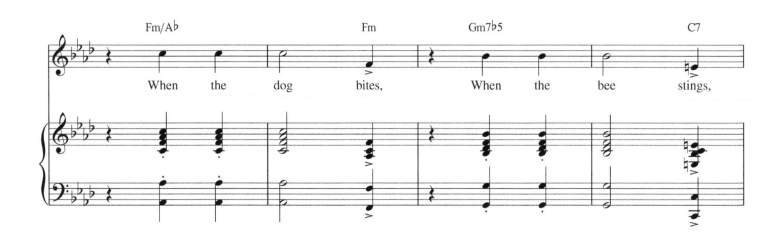

My Funny Valentine

BABES IN ARMS

Words by LORENZ HART
Music by RICHARD RODGERS

hold the way our fine feath-ered friend his vir-tue doth pa-rade. Thou

know-est not, my dim-wit-ted friend, the pic-ture thou hast made. Thy

va-cant brow and thy tous-led hair con-ceal thy good in-tent. Thou

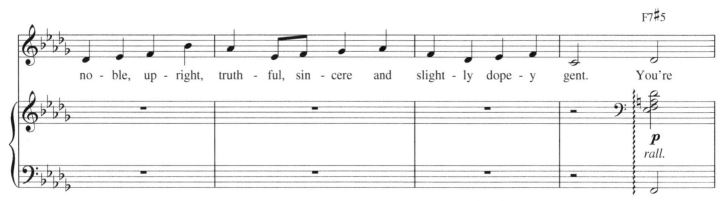

no-ble, up-right, truth-ful, sin-cere and slight-ly dope-y gent. You're

*The verse should only be sung by women. To begin the song without the verse, bar 4 of the introduction becomes:

My Romance

JUMBO

Words by LORENZ HART
Music by RICHARD ROGERS

REFRAIN
Smoothly, with expression

My ro - mance does-n't have to have a moon in the sky, My ro -

mance does-n't need a blue la - goon stand-ing by; No month of

May, no twin - kling stars, no hide a - way, no

soft gui - tars. My ro - mance does-n't need a cas - tle

My Heart Stood Still

A CONNECTICUT YANKEE

Words by LORENZ HART
Music by RICHARD RODGERS

No Other Love
ME AND JULIET

Lyrics by OSCAR HAMMERSTEIN II
Music by RICHARD RODGERS

How far a-way are you? How man-y lone-ly sighs, dear?

How man-y weep-ing skies, dear? How far a-way are you?

How long have I to go? How man-y moons to see, dear,

Nobody's Heart

BY JUPITER

Words by LORENZ HART
Music by RICHARD RODGERS

Oh, What a Beautiful Mornin'

OKLAHOMA!

Lyrics by OSCAR HAMMERSTEIN II
Music by RICHARD RODGERS

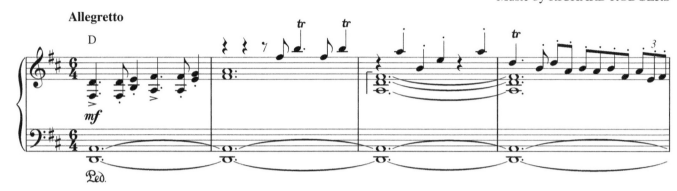

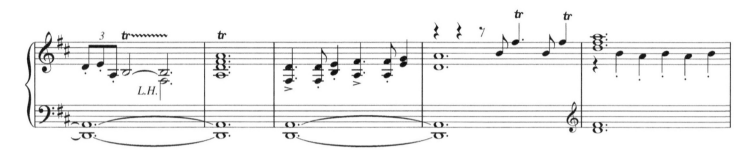

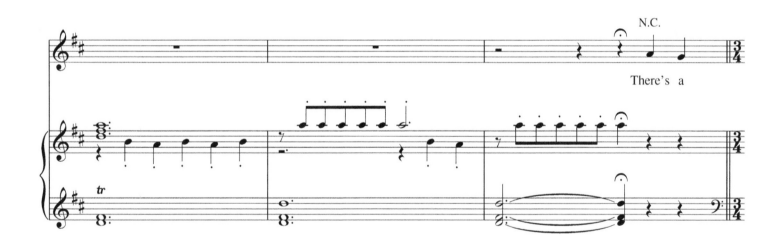

There's a

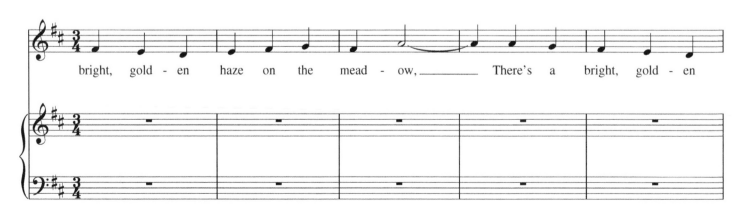

bright, gold-en haze on the mead-ow, _____ There's a bright, gold-en

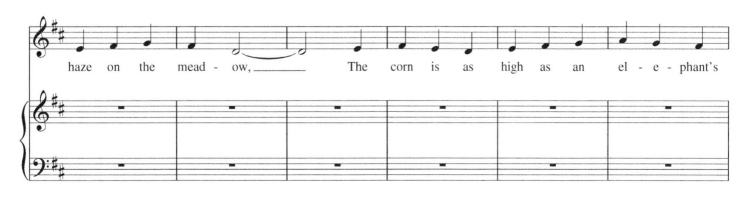

haze on the mead - ow, _____ The corn is as high as an el - e - phant's

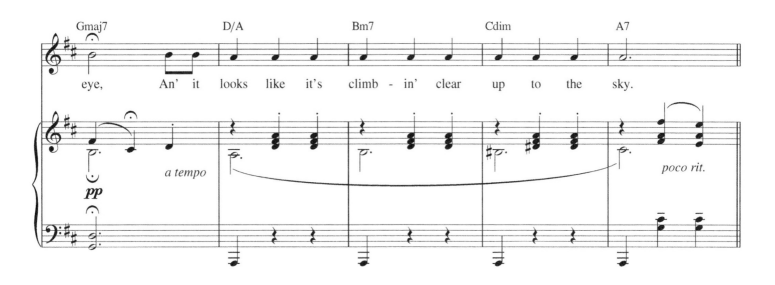

eye, An' it looks like it's climb - in' clear up to the sky.

Moderato

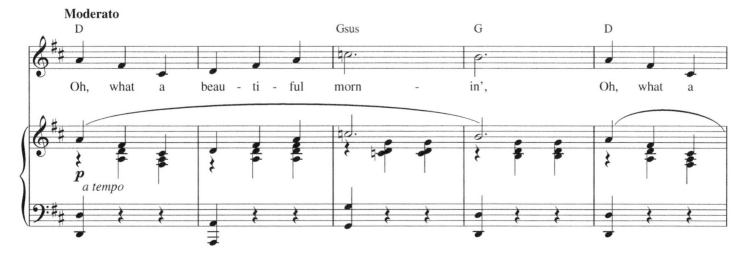

Oh, what a beau - ti - ful morn - in', Oh, what a

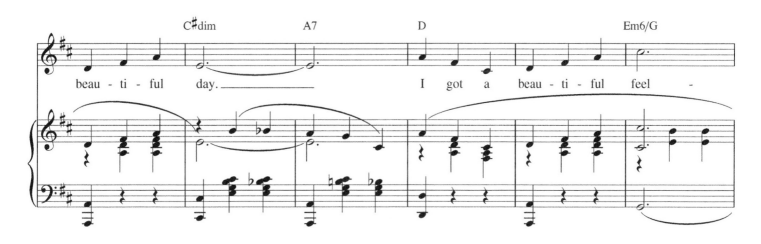

beau - ti - ful day. _____ I got a beau - ti - ful feel -

Soliloquy

CAROUSEL

Lyrics by OSCAR HAMMERSTEIN II
Music by RICHARD RODGERS

poco allargando

fat - bot - tomed, flab - by - faced, pot - bel - lied, bag - gy - eyed bas - tard will boss him a -

Poco più mosso

round._____ And I'm

damned if he'll mar - ry his boss - 's daugh - ter, A skin - ny - lipped vir - gin with blood like wat - er. Who'll

give him a peck And call it a kiss, And look in his eyes through a lorg - nette. Say!

People Will Say We're in Love

OKLAHOMA!

Lyrics by OSCAR HAMMERSTEIN II
Music by RICHARD RODGERS

Some Enchanted Evening

SOUTH PACIFIC

Lyrics by OSCAR HAMMERSTEIN II
Music by RICHARD RODGERS

then_____ That some-where you'll see her a - gain and a -

gain._____ Some en-chant-ed eve - ning_____

Some-one may be laugh - ing,_____ You may hear her laugh - ing_____ A - cross a

crowd - ed room And night af - ter night,_____ As strange as it

Something Wonderful

THE KING AND I

Lyrics by OSCAR HAMMERSTEIN II
Music by RICHARD RODGERS

The Sound of Music

THE SOUND OF MUSIC

Lyrics by OSCAR HAMMERSTEIN II
Music by RICHARD RODGERS

The Surrey with the Fringe on Top

OKLAHOMA!

Lyrics by OSCAR HAMMERSTEIN II
Music by RICHARD RODGERS

*The lyrics at these two spots have been altered just slightly for a solo singer version. The first line, sung by Aunt Eller in the show, is "Would you say the fringe was made of silk?" The bottom line, sung by Laurey in the show, is "Has it really got a team of snow-white horses?"

152

The Sweetest Sounds

NO STRINGS

featured in the Wonderful World of Disney's Production of Rodgers & Hammerstein's

CINDERELLA

Lyrics and Music by
RICHARD RODGERS

The verse does not appear in NO STRINGS, but was written by Mr. Rodgers for the song to stand alone.

Ten Cents a Dance

SIMPLE SIMON

Words by LORENZ HART
Music by RICHARD RODGERS

You're Nearer

TOO MANY GIRLS

Words by LORENZ HART
Music by RICHARD RODGERS

Time is a heal-er, but it can-not heal my heart, _____ My mind says I've for-got-ten you and then I feel my heart, The miles lie be-tween us, but your fin-gers touch my own, _____ You're

REFRAIN

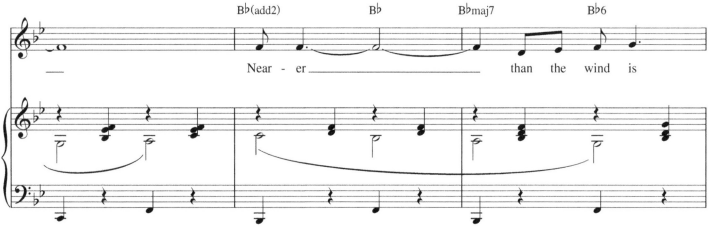

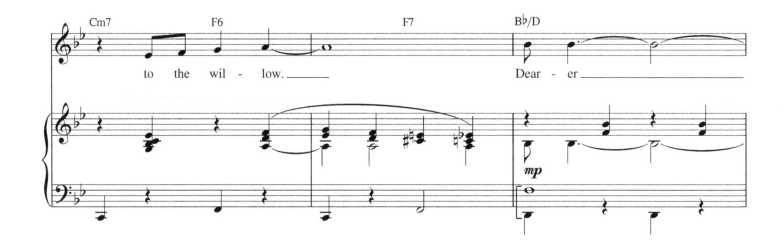

There's a Small Hotel
ON YOUR TOES

Words by LORENZ HART
Music by RICHARD RODGERS

This Can't Be Love

THE BOYS FROM SYRACUSE

Words by LORENZ HART
Music by RICHARD RODGERS

This Nearly Was Mine

SOUTH PACIFIC

Lyrics by OSCAR HAMMERSTEIN II
Music by RICHARD RODGERS

Tempo di Waltz espressivo

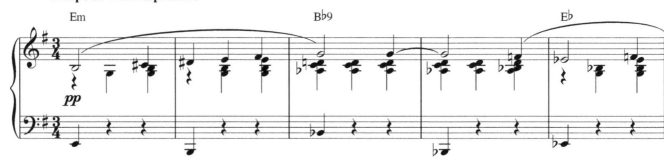

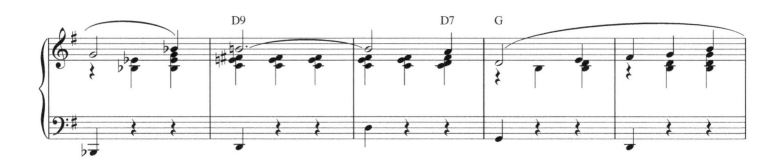

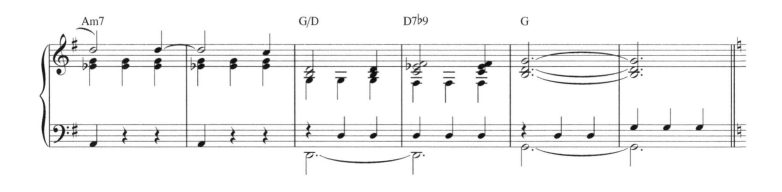

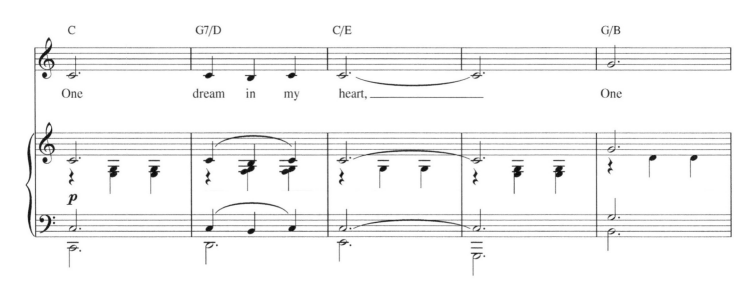

One dream in my heart, _____ One

Thou Swell

A CONNECTICUT YANKEE

Words by LORENZ HART
Music by RICHARD RODGERS

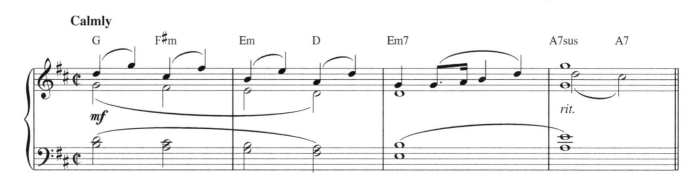

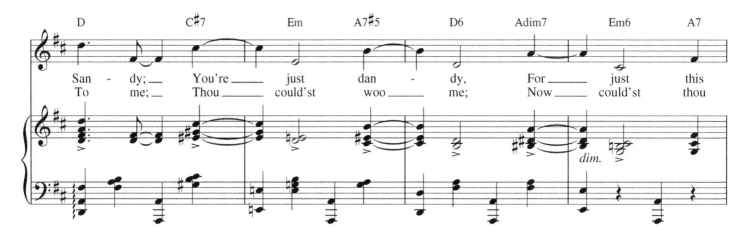

To Keep My Love Alive

A CONNECTICUT YANKEE

Words by LORENZ HART
Music by RICHARD RODGERS

Paul was frail, he looked a wreck to me. At night he was a hor - se's
Charles came from a san - a - to - ri - um, and yelled for drinks in my em -

neck to me, so I per - formed an ap - pen - dec - to - my, to
po - ri - um. I mixed one drink, he's in me - mo - ri - am, to

keep my love a - live! Sir Tho - mas had in - som - ni - a, he
keep my love a - live! Sir Fran - cis was a sing - ing bird, a

could - n't sleep at night, I bought a lit - tle ar - sen - ic, he's
night - in - gale, That's why I tossed him off my bal - co - ny to

Where or When
BABES IN ARMS

Words by LORENZ HART
Music by RICHARD RODGERS

With a Song in My Heart

SPRING IS HERE

Words by LORENZ HART
Music by RICHARD RODGERS

A Wonderful Guy

SOUTH PACIFIC

Lyrics by OSCAR HAMMERSTEIN II
Music by RICHARD RODGERS

You Are Never Away

ALLEGRO

Lyrics by OSCAR HAMMERSTEIN II
Music by RICHARD RODGERS

You Took Advantage of Me
PRESENT ARMS

Words by LORENZ HART
Music by RICHARD RODGERS

You'll Never Walk Alone

CAROUSEL

Lyrics by OSCAR HAMMERSTEIN II
Music by RICHARD RODGERS

Younger Than Springtime

SOUTH PACIFIC

Lyrics by OSCAR HAMMERSTEIN II
Music by RICHARD RODGERS